MEDITATION
A Treasury of Technique

Pam & Gordon Smith

MEDITATION
A Treasury of Technique

Photographs by Dave Phillipps

SAFFRON WALDEN
THE C.W. DANIEL COMPANY LIMITED

First published in Great Britain
by The C.W. Daniel Company Limited
1 Church Path, Saffron Walden
Essex, CB10 1JP, England

Reprinted 1994

ISBN 0 85207 214 7

Production in association with
Book Production Consultants, Cambridge
Designed by Peter Dolton
Typeset by Goodfellow & Egan
Printed and bound in Great Britain by
Butler & Tanner Ltd, Frome and London

Dedication
To Eugene Halliday, our Teacher and Friend.

Acknowledgements
To Vivien Worthington and Brian Netscher
for their help and advice

Also to the many teachers and friends with whom we have meditated over the years and whose meditations have undoubtedly contributed to this book, and to Marianne Gateley for typing and preparing the manuscript.

Contents

Introduction

The age old science of meditation renews itself in every age, presenting a new image fitting to the spirit of the age. Hence much in this book of ancient origin is presented with a new face, based on experience and insight gained through meditation.

Over the years many have visited us at Faith House and shared these meditations, some have come as seekers and spiritual aspirants, others have needed help in coping with the problems of stress and ill health. All, we trust, have received something of value, as will those who read and practise the meditations in this book.

Meditation has something for everyone, and has been proven by its adherents who regularly practise. It is increasingly recognised by the medical profession as a valuable aid in helping overcome stress-related illness.

For those who are sick, meditation provides a lifeline, it is a way back to health. For those troubled by stress it provides a way back to peace and equanimity, and for the confused in mind a means of achieving inner clarity. For the religious it strengthens faith, inspires hope and awakens the meditator to a perception of the Divine. Increasingly those who are sick, even the terminally ill, are being encouraged to meditate, as meditation can change the course of an illness. At the level of the cell, stress factors can cause a cell to oscillate and become confused so that it ceases to carry out its normal function.

Meditators can create the conditions within themselves necessary for health, pick up the reins of the mind and gradually guide themselves back to health.

For the person meditating alone or guiding a group, technique is all important. Books on the subject are few and far between and at the best only produce one or two ideas. Simplicity is undoubtedly the key, but we are all different and what is relevant and effective for one may not be suitable for another. Here we produce a fund of ideas, not necessarily to be kept to slavishly, but to awaken channels in one's own intuitive nature.

Meditation does not have to be a lonely affair only practised in the monastery or the seclusion of one's room. Far from it, it can be a shared experience as when meditating with a partner or within a group. This experience is of particular value when recovering from emotional or psychological problems or overcoming dependence on drugs, whether they be medically prescribed or otherwise; the group will provide the strength and support which is needed for the journey back to health and Self-dependence.

Not everyone is able to accept the discipline of the temple, or an order of monks, yet can still appreciate the wonder of life in nature, be inspired by the early morning light, or lifted to a perception of the Divine by the poet.

Many are the ways of man, we walk different paths and it would be ignorance to say to one, you should follow my path and no other.

There is no value in meditation if it means sitting for hours at a time meditating blissfully, while the grass remains uncut and the litter piles up all around. To be worthwhile it has to be transforming and bring realistic and developmental change within ourselves as well as be a positive force for good in the world.

Sri Aurobindo in his writings on "Integral Yoga" writes about the "Triple Transformation" which can occur if we meditate correctly. This transformation is brought about by a descent of the higher Consciousness and is experienced as Peace, Power, Light in the head, and eventually every cell within the body.

Meditation should never be static as it is about exploration, about discovering one's Self and in the process learning to cope. It is also about relationship with that which is of value, seeing and sharing with that which is true and beautiful, and in the process opening parts of ourselves which may have been previously closed. It is a continual process of awakening which is continued through the process of experiencing.

There is a story I remember of a man sitting out of doors meditating with his eyes closed, when a wise man came by and tapped him on the shoulder, asking "Why are you meditating with closed eyes? The day is beautiful and the sun is shining. Open your eyes and see God expressed in the beauty of the countryside."

The question is one very much of balance. We should be able to sit in the Sun and feel its warmth touching the body, catch the fragrance of the blossom, listen to beautiful music and still know the difference between the knower and the known.

Read the meditations in this book. Do not stick to them rigidly as they stem from many sources. If they create a flow of ideas and open a channel into an area of meditation unique to yourself and spiritually uplifting, they will have achieved their purpose.

Each of the photographs within this book is a meditation in its own right and should be used to awaken the spiritual within yourself. The photographer, Dave Phillipps, we feel is unique among photographers, as after university he took a job as Warden on Hilbre Island in the Dee Estuary. It was at this time that we were attracted to his remarkable photography, as Hilbre Island, twice a day cut off by the fast-flowing tide, provided the ideal vantage point for observing and photographing the land and sea birds and the seals which visited the surrounding sandbanks. David's camera undoubtedly caught some of the magic of the Island and Estuary, with its ever-changing mood of sea and sky. Now a professional photographer working with a wide range of subjects, he kindly agreed to provide material for this book of meditations.

The Truth Diamond

The concept of the Diamond Body comes from the Buddhist tradition and is a reference to the integrated Self, which because of the right sort of work has become an indestructible body of truth.

The diamond is a highly prized gemstone and the hardest of all minerals, and is prized for its purity and brilliance. It has now become a Universal symbol representing the inner diamond of crystallised Consciousness, which can be made ever more beautiful by affirming every truth within the mind of the heart.

Make a start with this meditation "The Diamond of Truth" by affirming every truth as you discover it, until you experience the reality of the indestructible within yourself.

MEDITATION

When waking or before sleeping look within the dark cave of your mind. See your thoughts as a treasure chest of gem stones. Select a diamond of the purest white, one which represents the highest truth. Place the diamond at the seat of Consciousness within the dome of your mind.

This diamond reflects the light of the Sun, and shines brilliantly with the light of truth, keeping the clouds away.

Every time you discover a truth to live by your diamond will shine ever brighter

The Golden Elixir

In ancient China there existed a religion of light and what to them was the Golden Elixir of Life (Chin Tan Chiao).

The Golden Elixir is a meditation representative of a spiritual alchemy which was used in an attempt to turn the base metal of their mortal body into gold, and by so doing achieve spiritual immortality.

Further details about this esoteric art can be found in the book "The Secret of the Golden Flower", a Chinese Book of Life translated by Richard Wilhelm with a commentary by C.G. Jung. Copies of this important book, published by Kegan Paul, Trench and Truber in 1942, can on occasion still be found in local libraries and second-hand book shops.

The meditation "The Golden Elixir" contains the essentials of this ancient mystical art, the rest is up to you.

❧ *Meditate in natural light with eyelids lowered. Offer no resistance to the light. Let the light flow gently backward as a golden stream.*

Encourage the light to flow inward with each breath, bringing peace to the heart. Offer no resistance to this light. Let it circulate and become The Golden Elixir of Life, and awaken The Secret Flower of your heart ☙

Candle Meditation

The living flame provides infinite possibilities for meditation and the safest and most economical way of doing this is to use a candle.

Sitting around a single flame can awaken in us the primordial instincts of the cave dweller, when it was fire that kept the wild animals at bay, and was the only source of light and heat. It evokes feelings of comradeship, friendship and security.

Some Yogis and Hindus still practise a fire ceremony (Agni Hotra), by meditating on the living flame at Sunset and Sunrise. This flame is produced by burning dried cow dung, as the cow is considererd holy. It is said to purify the atmosphere and help the meditator achieve harmony with life.

Here we use the lighted candle, which in churches throughout the world is used to represent living spirit. By meditating on and participating in its light you will experience warmth and peace.

❧ Meditate on the light of a candle flame. Then with love kindle a small light in your heart.

With each peaceful breath encourage the light to grow until it permeates your entire being. Then place the word Love in letters of gold deep within the light.

Letting go the word Love let it melt into the surrounding light, so that you are surrounded by an aura of golden white light.

Direct this light to friends in need and those you love ❧

For Strength

Affirmations or Governing Concepts are like New Year resolutions which, if they are kept, can help determine the events of your future life. Likewise dedication to a Divine principle will help determine the outcome of a meditation session, as it will any religious ceremony. This idea is far from new and I experienced it to excellent effect during a meditation period taken by Swami Shivapremananda, President of the Sivananda Yoga Vedanta Centres in Argentina, Uruguay and Chile. Some of the affirmations are as follows.

On the inbreath affirm – "Love is my real nature" and on the outbreath "not hate".

On the inbreath affirm – "Freedom is my real nature" and on the outbreath "not bondage".

On the inbreath affirm – "Truth is my real nature" and on the outbreath "not untruth".

On the inbreath – "Peace is my real nature" and on the outbreath "not disharmony".

On the inbreath – "Strength is my real nature" and on the outbreath "not weakness".

Affirm – Strength is my real nature, not weakness.

Then send your thoughts out to mighty rivers. Absorb their strength.

Reach out in feeling to the teeming jungles. Absorb their vitality.

Capture in a moment the ponderous strength of the elephant, the fierce courage of the lion, embrace the strength of a mighty tree.

Then lie on the earth, and move with the power which sends the earth on its journey round the Sun.

Affirm – strength is my real nature, not weakness

Quiet, Calm, Peace
and Stillness

*I*t was reading a letter written by the spiritual Sage Sri Aurobindo to one of his pupils, in which he differentiates the different levels of Consciousness in terms of Quiet, Calm, Peace and Stillness, which provided the inspiration for this particular meditation.

This meditation is also extremely effective if approached either as a guided relaxation, or as a technique to be practised at any time to relieve body and mind of stress. With a little adaptation it can also be central to any guided relaxation or meditation.

These methods are always very popular with absolute beginners, who need to be guided gently toward more profound levels of meditation.

For example the visualisation could be of a beautiful Zen garden in which a Master enters, exhibiting all the qualities of Quiet, Calm, Peace and Stillness. He then sits close by in order to share your meditation, and lightly touches your forehead, imparting a feeling of perfect Quiet, and when you are ready he lightly touches your forehead and deepens the experience to one of Calm, etc.

The letters of Sri Aurobindo are published collectively in several volumes by the Sri Aurobindo Ashram, Pondicherry, India.

❧ Place the word Quiet in your mind. Feel for the spirit of Quiet both within and without. Let the word "Quiet" fade from your mind, so that only its spirit remains.

Feel for the Quiet beneath any noise you may hear, underlying each breath that you take. Gradually become one with the spirit of Quiet.

Take the meditation deeper. Medidate on Calm. In feeling move to this new level. Experience Calm both within and without. Gradually release the word, so that only the spirit of Calm remains, Calm underlying every thought and every breath.

Take the meditation deeper. Meditate on Peace. Let it touch your heart, mind and breath. Peace fills your body within and without.

Finally step beyond all considerations.
Become Still ❧

The Disappearing Bowl

Here is what is essentially a Zen Buddhist meditation which is designed to release us from the particular so that we can experience the Universal.

There is much in Zen Buddhism that is worth meditating upon as the very nature of Zen is such that it quickly takes the aspirant beyond meditation to the direct realisation of the Self.

I was once intrigued by a Zen story which illustrates the spirit of Zen. It was of a monk sitting on a mountainside surrounded by his followers, it was the last moments of his life. A pupil asked him for a few last words of advice before he died. They were "Do not be deceived. Look directly. What is this?", and then the monk died.

Zen never allows you to be caught in the finite, but frees the Self so that it can awaken to its infinite possibilities.

❧ *Meditate on your body as an empty bowl. Feel the space within. Let the breath of life flow into this bowl, purifying and cleansing. Your bowl can contain all the stars, and anything you wish to put in it.*

Now feel Consciousness beyond the bowl, as that which gave birth to the bowl. You are the space within the bowl, not different from the space without.

Finally release the bowl to the space from which it came ❧

The Trouble Stone

I worked with and was taught by a spiritual adept, he was a great man and spiritual teacher, who did not seek publicity, but who did a great deal to raise the level of awareness of those around him. His name was Eugene Halliday. He said that there was no such thing as inorganic matter and that life was even in the stone, albeit a blind rotation of energy. It was Christ who recognised the ability of the stone to respond, as shown in the Gospel of St. Luke where the Pharisees asked the Master to rebuke his disciples. And he answered and said unto them, I tell you that, if these hold their peace, the stones would immediately cry out.

Let the stone help you with your problems and by so doing you may even awaken the life in the stone.

Find a large smooth stone, one that you can hold easily in your hands. Sit alone or with friends in a circle. Pass the stone slowly from hand to hand.

Give up your troubles to this S-T-ONE, the Self crucified one.

Cleanse the stone in free running water. Again pass the stone from hand to hand.

Give your love to this stone

Calm to Troubled Waters

Water has been for as long as man remembers a symbol for his emotions, even in dreams a wild and turbulent sea expresses agitation and disturbance at the emotional level. The closest link we have in ourselves with the emotions is the breath, this is why when we become emotionally disturbed the breathing also becomes disturbed. The rule then is "Calm the Breathing and Calm the Emotions".

Calm tranquil breathing is also representative of the still mind, the waves on the surface, the thoughts which come and go. These analogies and facts of life can be combined to produce effective meditations which can help relieve stress as shown here.

"Imagine that you still the surface waves of the mind until peace and tranquility descend into every part of the body, as if to the bottom of a deep calm lake."

MEDITATION

Visualise a rough sea.
Let your emotions and fears be the force which moves the turbulent waters.

Sit in the middle of this ocean.
Let your agitation peak in the waves that dance around.

Every storm must pass, so calm your breathing. Let your troubled waters subside until the breath is like a gentle zephyr breeze, with hardly a ripple on the surface of your emotions.

Visualise the Sun sending shafts of light through the clouds, which like Jacob's ladder join heaven and earth.

The waters, now at peace, recede into the distance.

You sit on the earth safe and secure

I Am

I AM is a poem which I dedicate to Bhagavan Sri Maharshi Yogi, whose message to modern man was that one should know one's Self, the principal means being the path of knowledge through Self enquiry. The form of the meditation and Self enquiry is determined by the all embracing question "Who Am I"?

The reality of the ubiquitous nature of one's Self is known to very few, but there is evidence that some of the holy men of the East have this knowledge and level of awareness, to quote a story I heard from a friend Sunder Chopra on his return from visiting the ashrams and holy places of India. A pupil at one of those centres gave his Guru a watch to express his devotion and esteem. The spiritual teacher accepted the gift, saying that he would wear it as a reminder, but on that wrist, then placed the watch on his pupil's wrist.

MEDITATION

I am the dawn that lights the sky.
The soft night air, the bedewed grass.
A lonely flower in a distant pass.
A Mother's Love. A baby's cry.
I am the strong and the straight.
The winding and turning of devious way.
A vaulted sky, a secluded bay.
A ploughed field, a wicket gate.
I am the silent and the free.
The infinite depth in an empty church.
The light of the morning Sun.
A loving heart. The knowing now.
I AM

Body Harmonics

*E*very form of life is a modification of power, that is power which vibrates and determines the patterns of life.

If we place sand particles on a piece of glass and bow the side as if playing a violin, we create sound vibrations which form the sand into geometric patterns. By not unsimilar laws our own bodies feel well and integrated when in harmony and distressed or in unsound health when disharmonious conditions threaten us.

Sound vibrations can exhilarate the healing of bones as well as disintegrate, as shown in some modern surgical techniques.

With this meditation, called "Body Harmonics", attune yourself to life and health by attunement to the sound vibrations right for you.

❧ Body Harmonics is the means by which it is possible to balance and harmonise every part of the body.

So visualise a temple, a holy place, which contains gongs, cymbals and bells. These are capable of producing the purest sounds possible. Imagine that you are meditating within the temple, when a holy man strikes first one instrument then another. First a deep sounding gong. Then he slowly passes on, producing sounds which become finer and finer. Feel these sounds vibrating, and harmonising your muscles, tendons and ligaments, then your inner structure for peak performance and health.

Finally with open hand he makes the sound of silence ❧

Levitation

It is not only the body which can rise up in an act of levitation, but also our spirits.

Physical levitation has been reported throughout the world from time to time, but there is no evidence to show that this is actually true. What is certain is that we can let heaviness fall away from the mind and lighten our load by attunement to the spirit of levitation.

MEDITATION

❧ *When depressed meditate and try to levitate.*
Let all heaviness fall from your mind.
Let tensions slip away from the body.
Feel the spirit of levitation
In each light and easy breath.
Become as a free spirit,
An unfettered body of light.
As darkness and heaviness fall away,
Merriment and laughter will rise up,
Lifting your spirits on high ☙

Become Like Christ

We have two minds, a lower mind a higher mind. The lower mind is programmed by the world in which we live and is necessarily imperfect. The higher mind, or level we associate with intelligence, is capable of visualising that which is perfect, such as the perfect triangle. It is when we try to draw or create that which is perfect that imperfections start to creep in. However we need the image of the ideal to guide our lives so that we continue to progress and improve the world in which we live.

The meditation "Become like Christ" makes use of the creative visualisation to provide the most perfect template through which to live.

MEDITATION

≈§ As you meditate
The most perfect Master sits close by.
His posture is perfect.
Gradually you adjust your posture to his.
Your hands become as his hands.
Your arms as his arms.
Your body and head mirror his body and head.
Your composure as his composure.
Your breathing and his breath as one.
He guides your understanding,
Love and Purpose,
Now and Always ≈

Peaceful Moments

To be Here and Now is to live in the moment – to be caught in time is to be determined by inertia.

To live in the Now Here moment is to be free and to be awake to that which is actually before our eyes, to enjoy the stillness of your heart, and capture the magic of the moment. The peaceful still moment, wherever you happen to find it, is always untrammelled by time.

MEDITATION

To experience Peace helps to freeze time, to hold the moment, as happens when we see something natural and beautiful, and hold its image in the heart. To experience Peace look for the beautiful and hold the moment. A flower opening, dew on the grass, capture the moment wherever you happen to be.

When exercising remain still within yourself, and view the body as a moving image, each unfolding stage of action a moment not to be missed.

Look for these moments of Peace in the moving picture of life

Become One With Nature

None of us is far removed from nature, we have our roots in the earth, we like being warmed by the Sun, and sharing nature's fragrance brought to us on the air.

To become one with nature is to be healed by the spirit of the tree, to be refreshed by the clear running stream, and brought to life by the clear morning air.

MEDITATION

❧ As easily as the mind can make you its slave,
Just as easily can the mind make you free.

Imagine that you meditate out of doors.
You are naked. In a secluded place.
The rain softly falls, making rivers on the skin.
Clear rivers which run away to the sea.
Your ears and eyes open wide to the gentle breeze.
Still the rain falls, making rivers on the skin.
Clear rivers which run away to the sea.
Let your mouth and tongue accept the clear waters.
A gentle breeze blows, whispering time away.
The Sun reaches out with myriad shafts of light,
Expressing itself as Joy in all things.
Take in the light.
Become the light ❧

Soul Breathing

Desperately the dying man who thinks that he has no soul clings to the breath which ensures his link with mortality. Yet he who knows that his soul is but a single zone of that infinite intelligence which brought him into being, trusts that he can only return to the source from whence he came.

Practise Soul Breathing and awaken to the infinite intelligence which is in you. Let it guide your every breath until you feel that you are not breathing but rather being breathed.

❧ *Watch your breath and calm your breathing until mind and breath become as still as the tranquil waters on the surface of a lake.*

From the centre will arise a subtle inner rhythm which gives rise to Soul Breathing, this lifts the breath as a flow of Consciousness (Puraka). As the breath turns from up to down comes the still natural pause, a period of assimilation of light (Kumbhaka).

Peaceful outflowing breath carries light and energy to all the cells of the body (Rechaka) ❧

Healing Visualisation

We all have a subtle template or spiritual blueprint, without which the body would soon disintegrate.

If we eat a carrot we do not become like the carrot, but break it down and re-assemble it according to the vibratory pattern unique to ourselves. Sometimes, due to stress, the pattern becomes distorted so that there is a breakdown in health. The healer, by recognition of the problem, can, by visualisation, re-affirm the way things should be, bring about a change in Consciousness and so assist in the healing process.

MEDITATION

Hold the image of the person who requires healing. Remember their every good quality, then see them in the mind of your heart as perfect.

When confronted with pain and suffering it is difficult to see much else. But perservere and continue with your visualisation until finally you see them in your heart's light as perfect.

In the person who is sick there will be recognition at a deep level of this perfect innermost structure which you have affirmed. They will then have a choice, whether to affirm this and return to health or not.

Do not be disappointed if it is not within the scheme of things for them to respond, but continue, as this will help them in the days ahead

Integral Meditation

An integral meditation is any meditation which brings us into closer relationship with ourselves so that we experience a greater degree of wholeness and have better co-ordination. By observing people we soon get some idea as to what we mean by a balanced person. For example, the head-stressed person is usually male, peers over his glasses, and engages in conversation in a logical and precise manner with little regard for the feelings of the person he is talking to. Those who are stressed at the emotional or feeling level often express themselves warmly, sometimes making contact by embracing, much to the discomfort of the head-centred being.

Next are the wilful type, who whether they know anything or not have little regard for your feelings, and may push you over if you get in the way.

All of these types, due to imbalance, are liable to create difficulties for themselves and others, whether it be headaches, palpitations or ulcers. We present here an integral meditation which will enable you to bring yourself into relationship at each level.

◆§ *To improve the integration of the three levels of your being, which are the Head, Heart and Will, first centre down to the Hara centre, which is a point two inches below the navel and at the centre of the body.*

With each outbreath repeat the word "Good".
Your Good being to Love the highest Truth.

Continue the repetition of the mantra "Good" for approximately five minutes, until the energy of your highest Good flows with each inbreath and outbreath, strengthening your whole body.

Next at the level of the heart:
With each inbreath affirm "Love is my real nature",
On each outbreath "not hate".
Continue for approximately five minutes, then change your mantra to "Love" on the inbreath, and "Love" on the outbreath. Let the light of Love fill the heart, bringing peace and light to the whole body.

At the level of Mind affirm with each inbreath "Truth is my real nature" and on the outbreath "not untruth". Continue your mantra for five minutes, gradually changing until Truth flows naturally with each inbreath and outbreath.

Finally let your eye become single.
Visualise your Good, Love and Truth as one light which links every level ও

Solar Cross

*T*he Solar Cross is a Universal Master Symbol. It symbolises the Cosmic Christ and among its many attributes it contains within it the symbology of the planets, which capture for all time the basic principles behind creation as well as some of the fundamentals within human nature.

There is the principle of Jupiterian expansion which is light and energy radiating outwards. It also represents Generosity and Jollity. Its opposite is crucifixion and Saturnine contraction experienced as withdrawal and depression.

These opposing forces find their resolution in Mercurial spin, sometimes seen as the winged messenger, or in the speed of the human mind. These forces which give rise to such rapid movement generate great heat and fire, as symbolised by the warlike planet Mars.

That which prevents the whole process seizing up and grinding to a halt, to become like a dried cinder in space, is Love as symbolised by Venus.

It is Love which provides the oil and makes the wheels run smoothly, the Sun representing the resolution of these forces as well as Cosmic Consciousness. This meditation briefly referred to here is very much for the adept, so we present an easier meditation with which to start.

❧ Meditate on the Solar Cross.

Feel your spine to be the vertical line of the cross and that you sit at right angles to time experiencing the timeless.

Look out onto the world and see this as the horizontal line representing time and the plane of existence.

The resolution of these two forces, that is initiative and inertia, is the circle of your influence. The circle can also represent your Karmic Wheel, every action creating a wave or ripple of energy through which we must steer the bark of this life.

Meditate to become as the vertical line of the Cross, free of inertia and Willing what God Wills for You ☙

With a Partner

*❧ Meditating with a friend or group
gives comfort and support, it
provides the energy to help
overcome weakness, and yet keeps
down to earth the ones who would
fly too high too soon. ঌ*

People need people, we can never learn by living in an isolated world of our own making. By sitting closely back to back with a partner you can quickly learn something about yourself.

It may be that your partner is warmer and friendlier than you are and that you need to adjust your attitude to life, or conversely the vibes you receive may be too low and on the heavy side, which may demand tolerance on your part.

Whatever the relationship, learn from it and try to achieve harmony at the highest possible level.

MEDITATION

*❧ Sit back to back with a partner, silently aware of their presence, your
spine straight and head balanced.
Though very much aware of your partner, maintain your integrity, and a
feeling of calm and peace.*

*Place your hands in prayer Mudra at the chest level, then as you inhale
take the hands up the centre line of the body and straight above the head.
Fingertips touch with your partner's. As you exhale take your arms out to
the sides, outlining a circle of peace and harmony around your bodies.
Slowly return your hands to prayer position at centre chest. Repeat three
times, then return to meditation seat with hands/arms resting on knees.
Share silently whatever harmony has arisen between you ঌ*

Merging Higher Selves

There are many levels of relationship. For some it is confined to the physical with an associated overflow of energy from the emotional level.

For others a significant relationship is an exchange of ideas, and for a few exceptional people it is at the level of the higher mind, the level we associate with Universal Truth.

This meditation "Merging the Higher Selves" is in the spirit of top level relationship with each meditation working for perfect harmony with a partner. It is at this level that we learn from each other at a subtle level, with a subsequent refinement of every level.

Sit facing your partner, fingertips lightly touching.
Enjoy calm peaceful breathing.
Gradually with calm peaceful breathing, with each inbreath lift the image of yourself still facing your partner to a position just over the top of the head at the level of the Sahasrara chakra.
Make both of your visualisations as perfect as you can, refining and perfecting the visualisation with each breath you take.

Finally embrace and enjoy the perfect interchange of your topmost energies.
Finally sit firmly on the earth, silent and still

Group Soul

This meditation "Group Soul" is much like the previous meditation "Merging Higher Selves" and is in the spirit of the Tantric tradition, where the right sort of relationship between spiritually motivated people makes possible reciprocal feeding at all levels. Forming a circle with a large number of people can be viewed as a chakra or energy wheel which has a lot of potential for healing and rebalancing.

When sitting in the circle you may feel that you are closed and insulated from the mundane energies of everyday life. Encourage this by feeling that the circle is open to a descent of the higher and more spiritual energies which promote healing and development.

❧ Sit for meditation in a circle facing its centre. Energise the circle by directing all your positive energies inward. We all have strengths and weaknesses, let the energies at your highest level fill the circle.

As the energy within the circle increases upon yourself to the positive qualities which you need for health and integration. Do not just be a receiver as there must be a fair exchange, continue to present the higher aspect of yourself, raising the vibrations of the centre.

After several minutes of attunement and re-balancing hold hands and sit in silence in a spirit of equanimity at one with the group soul, one spirit of awareness harmonising and balancing the whole group. Finally, release hands, and sit in harmony with each other ❧

Healing Mantras

Mantras have an ancient tradition indeed, stemming from both Yogic and Buddhist sources. They are essentially words which have ordering power and which help bring about change both physically and spiritually.

It is important that we know how to use mantra whether individually or in the group.

Yoga sources tell us that mantras repeated aloud (Jappa), are less effective than mantras whispered. But rest assured mantras intoned in a group situation can be very powerful and beneficial. Tradition and experience also tells us that mantras said mentally are more power-ful still and most powerful when part of the inner silence.

Mantras sometimes seem meaningless as in the case of some of the Bija or seed mantras used here. This is good as it strips them of any emotional charge which we may feel inclined to impose on them, as each letter of a mantra has its own level and function within the sonic geometry of the Universe and should be allowed to work without interference.

The healing mantras chosen here will focus and harmonise energy and promote healing in some of the most important areas of the body.

❧ *Form your group into a circle so that the vibrations of the mantras fill the space bounded by the participants.*

The first mantra is HRUM, a word that rhymes with room, and which produces a sound structure beneficial to the organs in the abdominal area. Start by placing the hands with fingers interlaced on the abdomen. Taking a deep breath stretch the arms forward – finally turning the hands away from the body.
On a long outbreath intone the mantra HRUM as the hands return to the abdomen, to focus as it were the energy of the mantra under the hands. Repeat the mantra three times.

The next mantra is HRAM which rhymes with calm.
The procedure is the same as previously, only this time the hands and focus are at the chest level.

The next mantra is HRAIM and rhymes with time. The hands and arms are stretched backwards and placed at the level of the kidneys. This sound produces a beneficial vibration for the kidneys. It can also act as a diuretic.

The mantra HRIM can integrate and harmonise the whole body. This time place the hands with fingers interlaced on top of the head. With a deep breath stretch the arms skyward. Then on the outbreath intone the mantra as the hands return to the crown of the head. Feel the mantra as vibrating down the central axis of the body from head to feet.

It helps to visualise colour in conjunction with the mantras:
Orange at the level of the abdomen.
Sky Blue at the level of the heart.
Violet or purple for the kidneys.
Golden white light down the central line of the body ❧

Absolute Breath

−Individuated Breath

Every letter of our alphabet has form and structure and is a precipitate of the energy of life which brought it into being. Each consonant can be considered as spirit personalised, and the vowels as pure energy which give life to each word. When we make a vowel sound we do not make a closure with the lips, hence vowels represent free unformed energy.

The study of mantra is a lifetime's work, and we only make brief reference to the important symbols used here.

The letter "H" is closely linked with the breath and represents spirit, it is also representative of a ladder which can have many rungs and represents the ability we have to establish a link between heaven and earth. The letter "A" in all alphabets represents the beginning and is a symbol for the Absolute. The letter "i" is a line pointing to a dot or a convergent point of spirit, and therefore represents individuation.

Keep the spirit of the mantra in mind when breathing "AH" and "IH" and feel yourself as part of life both Universal and finite.

MEDITATION

Finally attune yourself to the whole Cosmic field of life. The first sound is AH which symbolises Absolute Spirit. It is barely whispered, and felt principally within the subtle body. To make the sound raise the arms out from the sides and upwards. Feel the sound to be an integral part of the breath as you inhale and expand your awareness out to the Cosmos and beyond.

The next sound is IH and symbolises individuated Consciousness. It is felt to be a part of the breath. As the arms return to the sides you return in feeling to the level of individuated Consciousness.

Repeat three times, finally stand in silence as the Microcosm within the Macrocosm

*H*ealing Zodiac

*B*uddhists and Eastern mystics have throughout the ages used symbols and geometric patterns on which to meditate. These shapes, often drawn with mathematical precision, are called Yantras and provide a way of looking at reality. The Zodiacal Yantra used here is Sun centred, the Sun being representative of the immanent spirit, central to life, and which lays down the pattern of the Yantra, but does not get caught up in it.

Each sign of the Zodiacal Yantra represents a psychological type, or the stress placed on a particular human being. By placing a person on the centre we release them of any particular stress which may be imposed by any particular sign. The intonation of the most ancient name of God "OM" uniformly around the Yantra creates pure and harmonising sounds at every level represented by Earth (body), Water (emotions), Air (intellect), Fire (energic), which will help heal, harmonise and integrate.

MEDITATION

Ideally there should be 12 meditators, each representing one of the Zodiacal Houses, sitting in a circle facing inward, with the person who requires healing at the centre.

If this is not possible sit one on each of the Cardinal points with the rest on balanced positions around the Zodiac.

Yantric purification and balancing of the person at the centre is carried out by intoning the mantra OM three times at the levels of Earth, Water, Air and Fire, with the vibrations directed towards the centre. Helps are to inhale together, and on the exhalation intone the mantra OM in unison.

OM at the level of Earth is to purify the physical.
OM at the level of Water is to calm and soothe emotions.
OM at the level of Air is for mental purification.
OM as vibrating energy (Fire) is to integrate and calm the nervous system.

Complete by sitting in silence at one with the centre, which represents the higher Self

Each a Guru

*E*ach has within us that which is perfect and yet confined, much like a Genii in a bottle who can only peer out through a glass, in our own case usually a glass clouded by desires and imperfections. The rule is if you haven't a talent assume it, or if caught up in habit patterns, change in spite of them, this will help free the genius within yourself.

Here with the exercise "Each a Guru", we assume the highest role of teacher and guide in order to awaken to the highest within ourselves.

During meditation there should be a co-operative spirit which encircles the group, and holds it in its spell. This unitive spirit keeps out distractions, and gives a feeling of comfort and support.

With newcomers who are sitting for the first time verbal instructions may not immediately ease tension. Helps are in forming partnerships, preferably an experienced meditator with a novice.
Then each takes their turn, and adopts the role of Guru.

First the more experienced gives silent instruction in the art of sitting, by making gentle adjustments, balancing the head, lightly touching and easing tension. Then when good posture is attained both join in silent meditation. Before changing roles there can be a whispered exchange when helpful guidance is given.

Next allow the novice to be Guru to the more experienced meditator. This way there is likely to be recognition in the newcomer as to what constitutes good posture.

Using this method at the start of a session quickly creates a relaxed and co-operative atmosphere

Psychic Help

People who are ill often, in desperation, seek the help of a healer, and many, perhaps to their surprise, find that they do actually receive help, and in some cases are completely healed. Sri Aurobindo, a great mystic and teacher of recent times, in his Integral Yoga, wrote about the possible transformation of the physical body, and recommended that during meditation we look towards the Divine or the Supramental Power that can transform mind, life and body.

The highest role of the Guru is to help the students free themselves of the ordinary limitations imposed by the mental, vital and physical formations. As a teacher, if you can help bring peace, calm and purity to your pupil you will be doing a great deal in helping clear the clouds away, so that the inner light can shine through.

MEDITATION

In an established group in which exists a spirit of harmony there should be the sort of rapport which makes it possible for the group to work together, and each assist the spiritual awakening of the other.

This is best guided by a leader who is awake to each member of the group, and who knows when conditions are right.

The technique is for each to assume the role of mediator or guide between higher levels of Consciousness and the physical. Each mediator should visualise clearly the whole group. Then in imagination stand silently in turn behind each member of the group using the power of their concentration to open the Crown chakra so that it becomes radiant with light. Hands are then placed lightly on the shoulders while the power of concentration carries the light down to purify and lighten the heart chakra.

With this type of meditation can come the unmistakable feeling that something beneficial has happened, even though the receiver is not aware of the help of an intermediary

Crystal Healing

My first experience with crystals was with Dr Shri Ramamurti S. Mishra at the Faith House Yoga and Natural Health Centre on Merseyside. He placed between us and himself on the meditation platform a dark velvet cloth on which were several large beautiful clear crystals. The dark cloth seemed to represent the Cosmos in which the stars glistened and shone, and it seemed at the time that shafts of light reached out from the crystals to each meditator, enhancing the power of the medita-tion. Since then we have confirmed the ability of the crystal to amplify the power of the meditation, refine and strengthen one's per-ception when dowsing with the pendulum, and intuiting when working with several crystals that they can communicate with each other. We have come a long way from the days when crudely we used the crystal set to tune in to radio waves, and we still have a long way to go before awakening to the full potential of the crystal as a meditational aid.

≈§ *If with a group, sit in a circle to form a chakra or wheel, with a crystal placed at the centre of the circle.*

Concentrate on the crystal as a focus of spiritual light until the light gradually fills the room with positive healing light.

When the potential for healing has become sufficiently powerful send the healing energy to the person who is sick. Imagine that the crystal light fills the space where they are.
At no time should you feel that the energy flows from yourself, but that you are a channel for that infinite source of light which is never depleted ≈

Let Go and Let God

One of the most powerful healing techniques is to let go, free the spirit from the confines of the body, and let the healing energies of the Universe balance and harmonise the subtle body.

Usually dissociation of the subtle (astral) body occurs quite naturally during deep restful sleep, as it frees itself from the limitations imposed on it by the physical. However, many remain caught in their troubled dreams and awake to the day tense and unrefreshed.

Many of the Yoga techniques which give rise to the Conscious out-of-body experience are fraught with difficulties, principally because of the fear of letting go. The meditational and healing technique which follows is safe, as it provides a sure reference to earth through the hands of a partner, and will give the confidence needed to practise this technique of letting go and letting God.

Ideally a meditation Master should guide each step of the way, with your companion providing the assurance you may need by occasionally massaging each side of the base of the skull with gentle circular movements.

~ *Sit comfortably at the head of your partner at the same time as they lie outstretched and relaxed on the ground. Place your hands gently at the sides of their head.*

Feel that your partner is an extension of yourself, relaxed down to the ends of their toes.

If resting on the ground, feel the hands of friendship which offer you safe and sure support.

Gradually letting go, imagine that your feet float slowly up from the ground and that you rise high into the air, like a kite supported by its string.

Feel that you float free, high above the earth, and that your troubles blow away with the wind. Open your heart and mind to the healing forces around you, aware of the healing power of nature.

Open yourself to the far reaches of space. Let the healing energy of starlight into heart and mind.

You are the stuff of which stars are made. Return to your ancestral home allowing the higher knowledge of your ancestors to permeate your eternal mind . . .

Gradually, and in your own time, become aware of the safe supporting hands at your head. Slowly return to the earth like a kite drawn down by its string.

Become aware of your body resting on the ground. Take a deep, relaxing breath, then change places with your partner ~

Healing Partnership

The following meditations should be linked together, as they are most effective when they follow each other.

When practising the Healing Partnership we have found that two will silently join forces to help a third, as there is often one who will need the love and support which the others can give.

When practising the Zen Garden meditation the group leader should guide this or a similar sequence. Always let your feelings be your guide then your words will follow the right sequence.

If there is an odd one over when forming the partnerships make up a circle of four.

MEDITATION

❧ *Sit for meditation in groups of three, palms of hands lightly touching to form a circle, palms of left hands uppermost, palms of right hands downwards.*

Sit quietly in a spirit of friendship.

Support each other in silent communication.

Allow the energies to flow freely around the circle until, like water which has found its own level, you hold each other in perfect balance ❧

ZEN GARDEN – MEDITATION

❧ *Sit in groups of three holding hands.*

Visualise a tranquil lake within a Zen Garden.

Imagine each group of three to be as lotus blossoms, which share the stillness and peace of the lake, each meditator a petal of a lotus linked inextricably to the whole.

Become one with the beauty of the garden and the serenity of the lake.

Feel the lines of communication which hold each lotus in silent communication ❧

Colour and Visualisation

To heal is to make whole.
Pure white light is a symbol of
perfected Consciousness. Colour
is but one aspect of pure white light.

Through colour we refine our nature,
achieve balance, then, as if stepping
through an open door, enter
the True Light within.

Colour Breathing

Everyone appreciates the value of colour, which accounts for the care we take when decorating a room, as some colours stimulate and others calm. People also can be seen in terms of colour as some are red and vibrant and others grey and miserable. A colour therapist once told me that the colour green can reduce the size of a cancer tumour. There may be some truth in this, as individual cells in the body become agitated under stress, confused, and then not able to do their job properly.

Green is the ideal colour to soothe and harmonise.

Nature abounds with the colours which will heal the soul and relieve the stress of those of us who live in a world devoid of trees and the natural life of the countryside. It is most important that the city dweller takes advantage of what nature has to offer and, when visiting the countryside, simply to relax and let the colours of life flow inward.

❧ Sit at an open window, whether in a car or at home, breathe easily and naturally. If in the countryside look at the peaceful restful green of the fields or trees. Instead of reaching out with the energy of the gaze, relax and let the restful green flow into you. Avoid energising the world around you, rather relax and let the natural world energise you.

As you become calm and receptive select the colour vibration you need, feel this to be part of each breath you take, let the colour flow inward, harmonising and balancing.

When breathing colour into the body to harmonise and balance the energy of the chakras, breathe Violet, Indigo and Blue downwards into the topmost chakras; Green as if horizontally into your heart chakra; the colours Red, Orange and Yellow as if flowing up from the earth.

If you feel the need to focus a particular colour vibration place your hand at the level required, then feel the colour as flowing with each outbreath through your hand, healing and restoring balance to the energies of your subtle body ❧

The Rainbow Light

Imagination is not nothing, it is a certain amount of energy and form in a particular place. The imagination can form a vibratory link with whatever level we wish to communicate. Whatever visualisation we choose it is only a means to an end, a link with a particular level of Consciousness, valid until the time comes when we can dispense with the image and communicate directly.

The Rainbow Light can be used for both meditation and relaxation and is ideal for harmonising every level within one's self as represented by the entire colour spectrum of the rainbow.

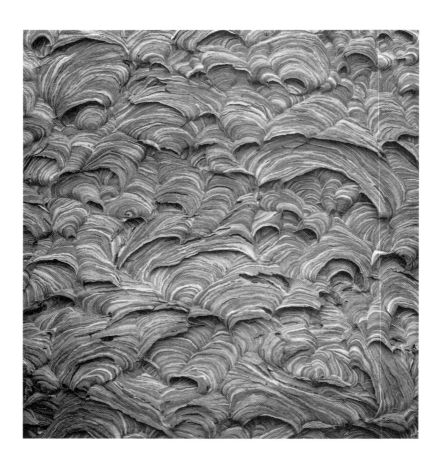

❧ *To restore Self Harmony when meditating, imagine that you sit in open countryside far from the madding crowds. Clouds slowly move across your sky with rain showers on the distant horizon. You are in the open and you feel as free as the wind. A beautiful rainbow lights the sky, and the Sun's rays seems suddenly to brighten the red end of its spectrum and your world is flooded with red energising light, which you absorb into yourself. It is powerfully strengthening and energising, builds stamina and endurance, improving circulation.*

Slowly the rainbow moves across the sky, Red gives way to Orange, which brings freshness and vitality to the world. You absorb this colour and its subtle chemistry as from a thousand freshly crushed oranges, so that life and sparkling energy flows through your body.

Imperceptibly the rainbow moves on until you are illumined by its beautiful yellow light, enriched in golden sunlight. The Gold light is a symbol of the Will and Purity. As you absorb this colour it strengthens your nerves, integrates and makes you feel whole.

Gradually the golden yellow of the rainbow gives way to the Green ray which illumines your world. Green is the colour of harmony, and is deeply relaxing. The most perfect green fills your aura, is carried inward on the breath, relaxing and deeply refreshing.

As you meditate the clouds slowly roll away from the horizon. The Sun's rays illuminate the blue of the rainbow light, highlighting the natural blue of the sky. This colour is deeply penetrating and healing, it flows through the pores of the skin, healing the body deep within, and bringing restful quiet to your mind.

As the rainbow slowly moves on, the Sun's light gradually brightens. The Indigo ray brings with it a feeling of integration and stability, so that you feel at one with the Self.

Indigo turns to Violet and Purple, and a deep tranquility touches your soul, and you feel very much at one with the Divine Will which expresses itself so perfectly in the world about you.

Finally you sit in silence at one with your maker ❧

The String of Pearls

–Chakra Meditation

*Restores harmony and balance
to the energy systems of the body.*

The meditation "The String of Pearls" is based on a Laya Yoga technique in which visualisation and mantra are used to raise the latent or suppressed forces in ourselves to a higher level.

There is a great deal of energy in every human being involved in worldly activities, which if they are not refined by spiritual activities, will at the end of a life still be drawn down and out towards the world and result in what could be a low level of re-birth.

We have here, while still keeping to the Laya Yoga and Tantric tradition, modified the technique slightly to make it more suitable for the Westerner.

We have called this meditation "The String of Pearls", however there is one pearl of great price which can only be achieved by a great deal of hard work and this is the pearl which represents the innermost Self.

We have discovered through experience that the benefits which come from meditating on the chakras are fully experienced on the following day, when there is mergence, and the energies of the higher levels have had time to settle down and re-allocate themselves and refine the lower chakras.

Visualise a string of pearls as lying along the spine, reflecting the light of the Divine Sun which lies like a beautiful crown of light above the head.

Within each pearl of light is a mystic symbol which links the energy of the chakra to the one Supreme energy of the Universe.

Muladhara chakra is the energy link which lies at the base of the spine. If you imagine that the spine is a cord along which lies a number of beautiful pearls, then the pearl at the end of the cord is the base or muladhara chakra.

Concentrate your attention on this base chakra and imagine that you look into the light of this lowermost pearl, and that deep within its centre it has a heart of gold. As you move closer to the centre you see that the light at the heart is reflected from a golden square which is the Yogic symbol for this chakra, Gold representing the colour of the Will, and the square stability.

This lower chakra with the one above can be the storehouse of a great deal of sexual as well as repressed energies. Start to work for control of this lower centre by first quietening the breath, then by breathing Peace and Harmony towards its centre. The square is a symbol for right-angled behaviour. Feel its strength and stability as a symbol.

Consolidate that strength by repeating its seed mantra LAM.

Swadisthan Chakra is some six inches above the base of the spine at the level of the genitals and this is the position for your second pearl of light. At its centre visualise a crescent moon against a dark sky. Imagine that the reflective light of the moon adds purity and lustre to the pearl which contains it. The moon is the symbol of the phasic behaviour of human nature. Feel that your crescent moon is always potentially full, and its light represents the purity of the soul reflecting the positive forces of Wisdom and Truth.

To integrate these forces at this level intone the Bija mantra YAM.

Manipura Chakra lies at the level of the navel, and the pearl on which to meditate here is white, tinged with a fiery glow which emanates from its centre. This area of the body is associated with energy and life. The Yogic symbol at the centre of the Chakra is an inverted red triangle. The energy of this centre when focused and expressed through its Bija Mantra RAM lifts the spirit and dispels depression. Repeat the mantra several times before moving on.

Anahata Chakra lies at the heart level and its pearl of light is a beautiful blue grey which reflects the colour of its central Yantric symbol, which is two interlaced triangles. The male triangle aspires upwards towards Truth and Wisdom, the downward pointing female triangle towards the earth and procreation.

When meditating on this chakra first become aware of the breath and its subtle inner rhythm, then move with the breath to the centre of the heart

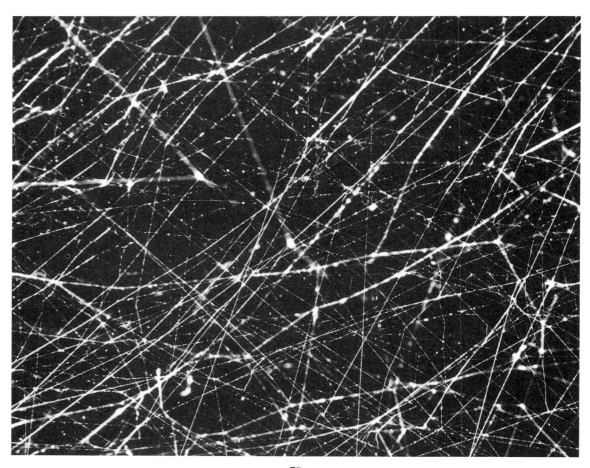

chakra. Continue to refine the breathing until you hear within the inward and outward flowing breath its Prana Bija Mantra which is "Hangsa". The Prana Bija Mantra will refine the energy of the centre, the Bija Mantra YAM integrates the energy of this centre.

Vishudda Chakra is at the level of the throat and it is here that we visualise another beautiful pearl of light. The Sufis have a saying, the purport of which is to let the Truth of your heart be on your tongue. When this is the case the light of Truth not only enlightens the heart, but also the throat chakra. Meditate on the throat chakra by visualising a white disc at the centre of the pearl of light, the disc representing the purity of Truth. Feel that there are no restrictions at this level, and Truth keeps you healthy and Free.

If you cannot speak the Truth – Remain silent.
The Bija Mantra at this level is HAM.

The Ajna Chakra or Brow centre is just above the centre line of the eyebrows and a little bit back, and the pearl here is the most penetrating yet as it represents the pure light of Consciousness which has within it a central harmonic, the mantra OM, which is the most ancient name of God. This command centre of the Yogis is experienced by developing an objective Self awareness, during which one observes with detachment the activities of one's own mind and the world around, all activities being presented to the pure light of Consciousness, which from itself determines whether to act or not.

Saharara Chakra is just above the crown of the head and is symbolised by a thousand petalled lotus which in reality is a lotus whose petals cannot be numbered, and which reflects the infinite creative possibilities of the Absolute. When meditating feel that this beautiful lotus actually exists, and that its light continually descends to illuminate, refine and bring health and light to all the lower energy centres in the body, which in themselves continually work to maintain the strength and harmony of the whole body ❧

The Stream of Gems

The Stream of Gems is a reflexive technique and colour visualisation which employs the backward flowing method, and in which light and colour are felt as flowing backward into one's inner space.

Gemstones are well-known healing agents, and if you have a favourite stone you can experience its healing power by holding it to your forehead and letting its healing vibrations flow back into yourself.

Another interesting method is attunement to the sound of colour, in which colour is visualised and felt as moving into sound and sound back into colour. This will help you through resonance to find the levels in yourself appropriate to each colour and so make colour healing more effective.

MEDITATION

❧ Sit for meditation and centre Consciousness in the Ajna Chakra. That is a little above the centre of the eyebrows and an inch back. In your mind place an image of a clear running stream by which you sit and meditate.

With image established and mind at peace, walk over to the stream and look down into its clear running waters. You see beautiful coloured pebbles over which the water runs refreshingly clear. Taking a pebble from the stream, you hold it in the palm of your hand and see that it is a beautiful coloured gemstone, washed smooth by the passage of time. You hold the stone to your forehead and feel the colour cool and refreshingly clear reaching back from the forehead and down into the nerve channels of the body, healing and soothing.

This is your secret stream of life to which you can return anytime, where the gemstones ever remain disguised as pebbles, keeping unsullied the healing power of their light ❧

The Apothecary's Shop

The generation of colour modules by use of the creative imagination is a powerful means of creating a healing atmosphere.

The more positively emotive the visualisation the better, as this will create a change of mood, with a resultant change in body chemistry.

Visualisation can take the form of light shining through the foliage of the trees to form a halo of green light around the body, or it can be the mental image of a stained glass window in a church, with its abundance of healing colours caught by the light shining through the saints depicted on the glass. A practical means of creating an atmosphere of colour is the use of the coloured lamps which are now widely available.

During your meditation let the colour of your choice permeate the Bio-field energies of the body, gradually relaxing and becoming still until the colour of your choice penetrates deeper into your energy field.

What follows is what can be called a positive emotive technique.

❦ Visualise an apothecary's shop.
In the window is a row of large pear-shaped jars which contain the
coloured liquid of an ancient art.

The light in the window illumines the jars which contain the hopes, the
longings for a healing elixir, of everyone who has ever gazed into their
bright colours. The apothecary for years has used the magic of the jars to
focus his healing arts.

Gaze into a jar, choosing a colour
appropriate to your needs.
Take your spirit into the centre
of the coloured light, its translucent
light bathing heart and mind as
with a healing balm.
Become as the light in the jar,
clear and bright, and a soul
trouble free ❧

Classical Meditations

Classical meditations have stood the test of time, and enable the meditator to experience the mystical by taking one step at a time on an ascending ladder of true and sure perceptions which crystallise the Truth of the infinite

Concentration, Meditation, Contemplation

To unlock the Universal from the particular is the aim of every meditator. To make this possible Bhagwan Shree Patanjali codified Yoga into eight limbs. This is a hierarchical structure which has its roots in the earth of sound ethical principles, its trunk constituting postural and breathing practices and its uppermost branches open to the light of heaven through meditative practice.

The topmost branches of this tree terminate in three distinct stages which are essentially parts of each other. These are Concentration (dharana), Meditation (dhyana) and Contemplation (samadhi), this latter at its highest is a Divine state and the pinnacle of the whole tree.

These three meditative stages are often confused by students. We have included them here in order to clarify procedure, show the relationship between each level and lay the foundation for sound meditative practice.

MEDITATION

First to define three phases of meditation which, with experience and practice, tend to overlap and flow together as Consciousness expands, and we grow towards true knowledge.

Concentration is the holding of the mind to one centre of interest.

Training in Concentration sharpens the mind, calms the nerves, and purifies the heart.
"Purity of heart is to Will one thing."

For your first exercise concentrate on the tip of the moving second finger of a watch. Each time your mind is distracted even in the smallest degree, stop and start again. First learn to concentrate for one minute. Gradually and with patience extend your time to three minutes.

Meditation unfolds from Concentration as a continuous flow of thought which can arise naturally and without effort, as if the centre on which we hold our attention unfolds, and tells its own story.

Once the mind has used its storehouse of mental information we can, if we are receptive, enter a second stage, in which is received intuitive knowledge from sources beyond mind. The dividing line between lower and higher meditation is indeterminate, as even in lower meditation the student will start to use his higher faculty of direct cognition.

Contemplation means with pattern, and occurs when we have exhausted our thought process during meditation, and our thoughts and feelings merge into one simultaneous act of comprehension, and with mind poised we see the whole picture as part of a meaningful pattern

Pyramid Power

*E*very geometric structure, whether it be a square, oblong or dome, has an effect on the way we feel. Some people can easily get depressed when in a dome shaped building, perhaps this partly accounts for the headaches and claustrophic feelings some people experience after visiting a planetarium. Other shapes, such as the church spire, represent the hopes and aspirations of the worshippers and guide their thoughts and prayers upwards. The pyramid shape, when built to a similar scale as that of the Great Pyramid of Egypt, has been reported to preserve foodstuffs and prolong the sharpness of a razor blade.

The pyramid shape, it can be speculated, was also known as an aid to the early Yogis, as excavations at Mohenjaro in the Indus Valley uncovered figures depicted in the triangular shape of the Lotus Posture.

The best way to prove to yourself that pyramid power can increase vitality, sharpen and integrate the energies within yourself, is to sit in a triangular posture, still the mind and centre within what feels to be the seat of power within yourself.

❧ To benefit from pyramid power we have to practise the Yoga of sitting and centre at the heart of the body's natural energy field, so that body and mind receive the benefit of abundant life and energy.

The posture we need to practise is one which maintains the body in a perfect triangular shape, as with Suhkasana or Padmasana.

By sitting in a stable position with a broad base and head representing the apex of a triangle, forces will be vectored in such a way as to focus energy at the centre of the body, about 2" below the navel.

Several articles and books have been written about pyramid power. Experience this power for yourself by sitting at the intersection of three vectors, one represented by an imaginary line down the centre of the body, the other two bisecting the angles at the knees formed by the base line and the lines from apex to knees.

Close forefinger and thumb in Gnana Mudra.
Quietly watch your breathing.
Centre at the seat of power, and meditate on the Here and Now ❧

The Centre Which is Everywhere

The practice of Concentration (Dharana) should be undertaken by everyone who aspires to meditation. Otherwise the uncontrolled mind will carry the practitioner along with it, often into the land of dreams.

This meditation on centering is Buddhist in origin, and not only helps with the process of stilling the mind, but can carry the meditator to a realisation of the true nature of the Self as he becomes one with the point of Concentration, and steps beyond the limits of the mind.

It is not everyone who can Concentrate and control the imagination to the extent of visualising a spot beyond the end of the nose,

often there are more immediate problems, such as aching joints, and the spot which demands to be scratched.

In a Buddhist temple once you have been given time to settle, and the bell or gong marks the start of the meditation, whatever distracts should become the focal point of the meditation, above all you do not move but remain calm and detached.

The same applies wherever you meditate, once you have set a time keep to it, and whatever demands your attention, rather than stop, use it as part of your exercise in Concentration.

⋅⋖ *Meditate on a dot which you imagine as just beyond the end of your nose.*

At first you will become aware of the dot as existing outside of yourself. Use your imagination to reduce the distance between yourself and the single dot, until you experience the sensation of mergence and becoming as one centre.

Then will arise the mystical experience of being at the centre of infinity, whose centre is everywhere, and circumference nowhere.

If you do not succeed, be patient. Helps are being aware of the breath at the end of the nose, the movement of air in the nostrils, not being

frustrated when nearly at centre, and suddenly finding yourself back where you started.

Patience will bring its reward, and the realisation that your centre is a centre which exists everywhere ⋗⋅

Tratakam

– Clearing the Vision

Tratakam or gazing is one of the kriyas or cleansing actions of Yoga. In the well-known Hatha Yoga Pradipika, which is an acknowledged standard text on Hatha Yoga, it says that one should stare at a small object, keeping the eyes steady until the tears begin to come. It also tells us that tratakam can cure all diseases of the eyes, which must, to say the least, seem a remarkable statement until one understands the subtle principles of gazing.

Tratakam can also be a preliminary exercise in Concentration as it requires discipline to keep the attention on a single object.

At the level of higher tratakam it is a means of extending one's field of awareness and awakening the higher intuitive faculties.

For example, when gazing at an Icon or symbolic object, there can be experienced an increase in magnetic field energy which gives a heightened sense of rapport, amplifies the sixth sense and provides the key to unlocking many secrets of an esoteric nature.

To achieve harmony both within and without, first steady the mind and then clear the vision by practising Inner, Intermediate and Outer gazing. This is the higher Tratakam.

Inner Tratakam is the awakening to the inner eye. It is a form of continual Self remembrance, an at-oneness with the Conscious Self which receives all impressions, yet is not caught by those impressions.

Start your meditation by becoming still like the hub at the centre of a wheel around which everything moves, but which in itself remains still.

Intermediate Fixing – Place an object on which to concentrate in the middle ground about eight feet from where you sit. Then direct your gaze in a calm contemplative way towards it. As an eye exercise the gaze would be held steady without blinking until the tears begin to fall. This is considered to be refreshing for the eyes. With the higher Tratakam at no time is there identification, only calm objective looking.

Outer Fixing – Extend your calm contemplative gaze to a distant object such as the horizon or a star at night. Without losing your inner stillness let Peace and tranquility remain part of your inner and outer worlds

Zen Walking

Walking Zen gives rise to the unique experience of remaining detached yet aware of every movement. It should ideally be a continuation of the meditative experience with each movement harmonious and flowing.

What in fact usually happens with the beginner is that movements are clumsy and disjointed rather than flowing. This is usually because there is thinking about walking rather than letting the moment express itself in movement. It is not unlike running downstairs, if you stop and think which foot goes next you are liable to trip and fall, yet if you let it happen you seem to glide down the stairs. The important difference with Zen is that the movements are not mechanical but wholly Consciousness without losing any of their fluidity.

Zen walking requires that you be aware of your contact with the ground, the moment a foot leaves the ground, and every detail of the synchronised movements of your body, with each movement unfolding into the next.

The final stage comes when there is attunement not only with the body but with everything around you, your walking does not offend nature and there is the sense that the air, sea and sky and everything that should happen to be around you is sharing your experience.

Do not be disappointed if things do not happen immediately, persevere and hold each moment until timeless movement holds past and future in a simultaneous act of comprehension.

ᵥᵨ *Contemplative walking can provide the relief needed after long periods of sitting. It also provides the means of continuing the spirit of meditation at the same time as enjoying gentle exercise.*

Prepare for walking by placing hands together with the back of one hand resting on the palm of the other and the thumbs lightly touching. Then start to walk slowly, fully aware of the function of walking. There should be no aspect of walking which escapes your attention, heel touching, sole of the foot, etc. There should also be awareness of the breath, which is peaceful and co-ordinated. In the hands you can visualise a symbolic golden ball which symbolises the Will to Self Realisation. Alternatively feel that it is Peace or Love which rests in your hands like a lotus blossom, and that as you walk the spirit of Love becomes a part of your every movement ᵨᵥ

Motive

Motive is movement or action of the Will, the Will being the Power in us which can initiate any particular action or movement.

It is not easy to remain Consciously in control of one's life, it is much easier to get caught up in things already started and just drift along with them.

For most of us any initial act is analogous to pushing a boulder down hill, which when once started is difficult to stop.

To overcome inertia in our lives and keep to the direction in which we wish to go it is necessary to practise continual Self remembrance and remain in a position from which control is possible.

Meditation on Motive is about discovering how much inertia you have in your life and to what extent you are free and in control of events.

MEDITATION

This is where, in an objective way, we discover the truth about ourselves without making any excuses or trying to justify anything we do.

Many of the decisions we make in life are because we believe through education or family upbringing that it is the correct thing to do.

Try to look at yourself and be clear about motive

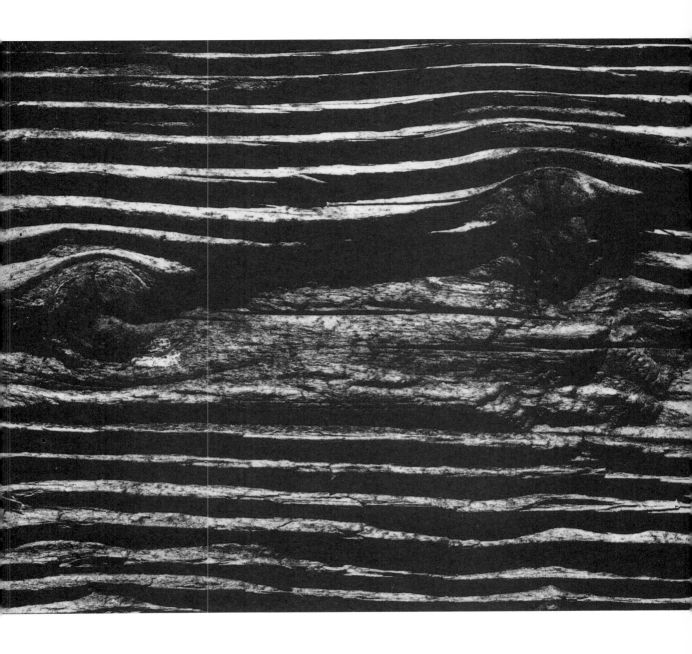

Things As They Are

It is possible for meditators to get caught up in a sense of euphoria and to continue meditating while the birds build their nests around them, the rubbish piles up, and neighbours view them as some sort of curiosity.

There is no point to meditation unless it brings beneficial change, that is both to the individual and to the world at large. It is above all necessary to develop a sense of realism. It is not good enough just to say "Come in, the water's lovely". Meditation on things as they are gives a sense of reality, awakens us to the true and factual and helps us build on a safe a secure foundation.

❧ The rule for this meditation is to cultivate the habit of seeing things just as they are, without any emotional overtones. This means in a sense that if you meet a ghost you measure it.

This technique reduces fantasy to fact, which is most essential when practising any form of meditation. When meditating on an object, try holding it in your hands and observe that whatever it is, it is contained within itself, and that by using words to describe it we are limited by the application of the terms we use, and the object still remains what it is no matter how eloquent the words we use to describe it.

Try to develop wholeness and realism when looking at things. For example, ask yourself "Why am I meditating? What are my true beliefs, and who gave them to me?" Analyse the things you have done during the last 24 hours, and to what extent you were in control. Meditation is about discovering yourself and overcoming past inertias, so that decision making is free and spontaneous, and brings new light on the things we do. We are born, we grow, we work and we die. What is it all for?

To discover whether or not you are in control of your life, on retiring reflect on the pattern of each day's events. If you start at the beginning of the day you will tend to pick up the trend of its habitual pattern and re-inforce it. So start where you are and go through the day in reverse. This way you will unlock the inertia involved in your decision making.

Remember, accept nothing at face value until you have examined it thoroughly. Always try to cultivate a spirit of realism. The following meditation on "Things as They Are" is a continuation of this spirit of realism ❧

Om Mani Padme Hum

Lama Govinda Anagarika Govinda, in his illuminating book "Foundations of Tibetan Mysticism" structures his writing around The Path of the Great Mantra – "Om Mani Padme Hum". He writes that the meaning of such a mantra cannot be exhausted by its component parts, the whole being more than the sum of its parts.

This is very true as analyses of the mantra or endless repetition is unlikely to bring enlightenment. This is particularly true of the Great Mantra as it is not something to use to produce a particular effect as it is an expression of, and points to, that which is central to creation, the Universal Self.

When using and being guided by the spirit of the mantra we have to transcend ego and make the transition from something we use to something we become: The Jewel in the Lotus of Life.

MEDITATION

❧ The Jewel in the Lotus (Om Mani Padme Hum) is a well-known Tibetan Mantra which, if repeated with understanding as to its meaning, will bring a sense of happiness and liberation.

Om – the most ancient name of God, the Absolute Good which is without limit, yet complete in itself.

Mani – The Atman (Self) is a beautiful inner Jewel or Diamond, which reflects the true nature of the Divine Sun.

Padme – Lotus or play of light, which is a symbol of spiritual unfoldment, and which embraces the diamond of Truth at its heart.

Hum – The sound combination which carries and embodies the spiritual power of the mantra in every part of the body, and which makes possible the transformation of the physical ❧

The Diamond Body

The Diamond Body is the result of pressure and the facing up to those pressures in a spirit of optimism. The salmon could not possibly reach his spawning grounds by not facing up to the strong currents and forces which oppose him. Likewise the humans will never discover themselves or be re-born to the indestructible Self by being swept away by every difficulty which confronts them.

It is truly said that opposition is true friendship, as without it we could not discover our true nature and those facets which enable us to shine.

Life is a testing ground which should test to destruction, but only those things which are not eternally true, so that the innermost diamond of truth can shine in all its glory.

❧ Crystallisation at the spiritual level of all that we hold True is referred to as the Diamond Body. It is a body of light which as such outlives the physical body.

To build for ourselves a body of light we have to live by the highest principles, integrating eternal values. Helps are first to discover your spiritual name. Your spiritual name then becomes a nucleus undistorted by false values, on which you can build. As your Diamond Body grows ever brighter your physical body becomes secondary, until it is only like dust which is finally blown away from the mirror of the eternal ❧

Find Your Spiritual Name

Not everyone understands or grasps what is meant by the Self or what it is to be Self realised, as the Self is beyond limitation except when it falls into identification, and then it comes under the law of whatever it identifies with. Our parents and educators, no doubt from what they considered to be in our best interests, tried to make us fit a mould or pattern, either to become good citizens or upright members of society.

It is only when we choose to become "Self" responsible that we are likely to choose a spiritual name, as this represents a new beginning and symbolises being re-born.

When this time arrives and you discover your spiritual name it has to be kept secret as it is sacred to you. Do not be in any hurry to disclose any new found truth that you think worthy to be affirmed in that name, as it first should be given time to modify your nature.

Also very truth is not ready to be accepted by the world at large.

Matthew 7:6 Give not that which is holy to the dogs, neither cast your pearls before the swine, lest they trample them under their feet, and turn again and rend you.

The higher knowledge obtained from meditation modifies nature, affects looks and behaviour, and gives a new spiritual identity, so that there is a sense of being re-born.

Yoga and meditation students often affirm this new identity by either adopting Sanskrit names, or accepting a name conferred upon them by a Guru. The purpose of such a name is to mark a new beginning, shed the old identity, and with it the accumulation of emotional charges and erroneous ideas which have attached themselves to the label, which they have carried with them since birth.

To find the spiritual name which is right for you, a name neither tied to East or West, but which has its own unique place in the sonic geometry of the Universe, we have to meditate on the letters of the alphabet. First the consonants, which represent formal sound structures which bring sound into existence. The vowels, which are kept to one side for the moment, are made without closure of the mouth, and represent unformed spirit.

First take each consonant, starting with the letter "B", and feel for the vibrational rate which each letter represents. It will be found that some letters you will like and others you will not. Reject all the letters you do not seem to have an affinity with. Continue this process of meditation on each letter until left with only three or four consonants. Next take the vowels, which represent free spirit, selecting one or several of these, and introduce them to the consonants so that they are given a soul and hence meaning. This is your spiritual name ❧

Nada Yoga

– The Yoga of Listening

Nada Yoga, the Yoga of listening, has been from the earliest times a reference to the mystical or inner sounds which can be heard during this form of meditation. These sounds are referred to in the Hatha Yoga Pradipika, and to quote a few lines from these early Sutras:

> "Yogis who practise Samadhi (Contemplation) on those internal sounds experience an indescribable joy."
> "The Muni (Sage) should close his ears with his hands and fix his attention on the internal sounds until he attains the state of perfect stillness."
> "At the beginning of practice various sounds are heard, and as practice continues subtler and higher sounds are heard."

The Pradipika also describes the type of sounds which are heard, such as the sounds of the ocean, small drum, a conch, a bell and a gong.

This type of meditation will appeal to the mystic and is begun by concentrating on external sounds, then inner sounds, finally selecting only subtle sounds until eventually the mind gives up all its activity and perfect calm is experienced.

For many people sounds heard within the ears are an unwanted phenomenon and listed under the well-known medical condition "tinnitus aurium". It may be that some of these sounds are more than just a malfunction of the hearing system, as a remarkable theory was put forward by Yogi Dr Ramamurti Mishra, who was our guest at the time. He said that much of that which we call tinnitus or ringing in the ears is the result of psychic or higher levels of Consciousness and that they should be meditated upon, as it is most likely that a change of direction is needed in our lives.

With the meditation on listening we have introduced here, we bring the art through centuries of time and very much up to date, as much that we have heard in this life and through our ancestors still plays its tune. This we need to examine, reject or integrate a technique which, when learned, we can continue to use when reaching into the realms of the mystical.

To gain inner clarity we have to leave no stone unturned, but work continuously to bring all to the full light of Consciousness. There is a great deal which our minds have accepted blindly and without question – to obey unexamined knowledge is to be much like a robot with no will of its own. Through meditation we can clear away the rubbish, and only retain that which is worth keeping.

With spine straight and body poised, sit with a still mind and listen. Gradually the stillness will permeate the entire body, and there will be less pressure to keep thoughts which are deeply hidden out of sight. If you continue to listen you will hear sounds, they will be the sounds of your ancestors and past teachers telling you things, the sounds will rise to the surface like bubbles rising to the surface of a pool.

Many of the things you hear you will agree with, and others not. Some things will be said with great authority, none the less examine them all, and say to yourself, do "I" really believe these things? If so, and they stand the test of your Conscious examination, affirm them, make them your own, and keep them close to your heart. If not, throw them out, and by so doing avoid the second death, which will be the death of all your unrelated ideas. By so doing you will be born again in this lifetime to all that is Universally True

*I*ntrospective Breathing

– *Pali Texts*

*T*his meditation on Introspective Breathing we have taken from one of the earliest known literary sources of Buddhism in the Pali Canon, which tells us that in order to find that which is of the highest value we have to transcend mind and become more closely aware of the nature of Consciousness.

The first verse of the Dhammapada in the Pali texts, begins with the words "All things are preceded by mind, led by the mind, created by the mind".

The essence of Buddhism is the attainment of perfect knowledge and liberation, one way to liberation being meditation on introspective breathing in which the breath becomes the vehicle for spiritual experience and forming the link between body and mind.

The Conscious observation of inhalation and exhalation is that which causes the unfoldment of the four foundations of Mindfulness (Satipatthana), the seven factors of enlightenment (sambojjhanga) and, finally, the perfect knowledge and liberation.

First steps constitute: the simple awareness of breathing, without impulse or mental interference from the mind. Hereby breathing becomes Conscious and the organs through which it flows.

The Pali text also says that, after the meditator has retired to a lonely place and has taken the traditional position of meditators, he Consciously breathes in and out, etc. . . . .

◄§ Sit for meditation – Consciously breathe in and out.

Drawing in a long breath, he knows "I am drawing in a long breath".
Exhaling a long breath, he knows "I am exhaling a long breath".
Drawing in a short breath, he knows "I am drawing in a short breath".
Exhaling a short breath, he knows "I am exhaling a short breath".
"Experiencing the whole body I will inhale."
"Experiencing the whole body I will exhale."

What is meant by experiencing the whole body is the subtle body. Feel as if the pranic breath fills the inner temple of your being, the breath not confined by the lungs.

"Experiencing serenity I will breathe in."
"Experiencing serenity I will breathe out."
"Experiencing bliss I will breathe in."
"Experiencing bliss I will breathe out."
Continue to practise until your breath becomes a vehicle for spiritual experience.

Continue Consciously, and experience mental activities, gladdening the mind, concentrating the mind, freeing the mind.

Repeat I "Will" inhale and exhale ॐ

The Four Brahma Viharas

(Divine States)

The Four Brahma Viharas or sublime moods are also subjects mentioned in the writings of the Pali Canon and have come to occupy an important position in the field of Buddhism. They are not strictly meditations as they belong to the field of the higher emotions rather than the mind.

The following quotation from the Maha-Sudassana Sutta summarizes the nature and purpose of the exercise.

"And he lets his mind pervade one quarter of the world with thoughts of Love, with thoughts of Compassion, with thoughts of sympathetic Joy and with thoughts of Equanimity; and so the second quarter, and so the third, and so the fourth. And thus the whole wide world, above, below, around and everywhere does he continue to pervade with heart of Love, Compassion, Joy and Equanimity, far-reaching, great, beyond measure, free from the least trace of anger or ill-will."

In the Love meditation the meditator sends Love as it were into the world around him, Compassion then looks down towards the world and all its suffering, Joy is the emotion which looks upward to the world of happiness, finally Equanimity restores the harmony disturbed through self-identification with these two extremes.

ᴥ LOVE – meditate on Love without any restrictions.
Suffuse your whole being with Love.
Attune yourself to Love at its highest – that is the power which works for
the development of the full potentiality of all beings.
Become as the spirit of Love, and radiate Love to all around you, both to
friends and enemies alike.

COMPASSION – represents eternal harmony which arises from
understanding Love.
Attune yourself to the All Compassionate One that is the Buddha. Become
as the Enlightened One, and look down to the world of suffering with
utmost Compassion.

JOY – to be joyful is to be happy,
and it affirms the situation you are
in. Be happy for other people and
their success, but at the same time
look within yourself for any trace
of jealousy. Feel that other people's
happiness is your happiness.

EQUANIMITY – is serenity and
composure which comes from
detachment. Composure in an
angry man is impressive. Develop
a constant and unwavering
steadiness of heart in all
circumstances, whether
unfavourable or favourable.
After passing through Love,
Compassion and Joy return to the equilibrium of your innermost spirit ᴥ

Patanjali's Yoga Sutras

*B*hagwan Shree Patanjali's compilation of Yoga Sutras is rich in short significant statements, each one provides food for thought, and needs time for reflection and meditation.

The Sutras are the results of many years of profound study, each one forming the central hub of a much larger body of thought. There is nothing mechanical about these precise word symbols presented by Patanjali, only Conscious thought at the highest level could have produced them, and only Consciousness itself will reveal the truth about each statement. To the Sage and Mystic it is only Consciousness or Sentient Power which we call life that can crystallise and synthesise existence into meaningful patterns, providing its own vehicle of Self expression.

Consider one of the Sutras which Patanjali presents for meditation:

"Concentrate on the Pole Star;
know the motion of the stars".

To the serial thinking mind such a statement would seem absurd, as only the higher or intuitive mind has the breadth and vision to unlock the secrets of the Universe.

Patanjali recognised the limitations imposed by mental activity, as his first leading Sutra states simply and directly:

"Yoga is controlling the activities
of the mind (chitta)".

The word Yoga is the same in spirit as the word religion as it means Union in the sense of binding back to the source of all life in our selves. Stilling the mind is a bit like the clouds clearing away from the Sun, or the surface waves on a lake becoming still, which enable us to see the bottom much more clearly and much that was previously hidden from view.

When meditating on the Sutras presented here, let them create their own picture without interference from your mind, and gradually each will reveal what it has promised.

❧ Concentrate separately on the word, the meaning and the object which are mixed up in common usage; understand the speech of every creature. Concentrate on the impressions of the past; know past lives. Concentrate on another's mind; know that mind.

You cannot know its contents unless you concentrate on those contents. Concentrate on the form of your body, suspend the power of another to see it, and as the light of his eye cannot reach you become invisible. Concentrate on immediate or future karma; know the time and cause of death. Concentrate on friendship, mercy, joy; excel in them.

Concentrate on strength like that of the elephant; get that strength.

Concentrate on inner light; know the fine, the obscure, the remote.

Concentrate on the Sun, know the world.

Concentrate on the Moon, know the planets.

Concentrate on the Pole Star; know the motion of the stars.

Concentrate on the navel; know the organism of the body.

Concentrate on the hollow of the throat; go beyond hunger and thirst.

Concentrate on the nerve called Koorma; attain steadiness.

Concentrate on the light in the head; meet the masters.

Concentrate on intelligence; know everything.

Concentrate on the heart; know every mind.

Sensation is the result of identification of Self and intellect; they radically differ from each other, the latter serving the cause of the former; concentrate on the real Self; know that Self ❧

Mantra Om

There is a great deal of mystery surrounding the sacred Mantra OM. Many have tried to unlock its secrets yet always there will remain more to be discovered. The earliest references we have to the Mantra OM are in that part of the Vedic writings called the Upanishads, the oldest of which were composed between 800–400 BC. The most concise explanation is found in the short Mandukya Upanishad which commences with the words.

"OM. This eternal word is all:
what was, what is and what shall
be, and what is beyond is in eternity.
All is OM".

The word pronounced OM is broken down into three syllables A.U.M. A is referred to as waking consciousness, U is dreaming consciousness, M is sleeping consciousness.

Such is the reverence attached to this Divine word, that it is seen as no less than the creative word of God, and that which represents the Power which orders creation.

Christians equate the word with that which is referred to in St. John's Gospel, ch.1, v.3.

"In the beginning was the Word, and the Word was with God, and the Word was God. The same was in the beginning with God. All things were made by Him: and without Him was nothing that was made."

We cannot do better here than to dedicate and equate the Mantra OM with the Holy Trinity, that is the triune nature of God as understood by the Western and Christian mind. The trin-

ity has a direct relationship with man mortal and Divine, we use the mantra here as a means of awakening the three parts of man to that spiritual level where he belongs.

❧ OM, the most ancient name of God, represents that which is without limit, yet complete in itself.

Start your mantric repetition with a deep inbreath, and on the outbreath let the sound of the mantra vibrate throughout your body, reaching out to the skin surface and beyond.

Dedicate the mantra OM to Omnipotence, the generative power of all life. After an inbreath intone the mantra deep within yourself at the level of Will, OM representing the All Powerful.
Understand Christ's statement
   "I and my Father are one."

Dedicate the mantra OM to Omniscience, the All knowing One, OM representing the Divine Word or Logos. Harmonise your mantra with this principle of Truth.
Understand Christ's statement
   "I am the Truth."

Dedicate the mantra to Omnipresence, the ever present and sustaining life principle. Here and Now.
Understand Christ's statement
   "I am the Life."

Finally dedicate the mantra OM to understanding its triune nature in one act of comprehension, and Christ's
   "I am the Way (Will), the Truth (Logos), and the Life (Love)." ❧

Chakra Meditation

The word "chakra" is a Sanskrit term meaning a "wheel" or centre on the spine governing a group of functions. Some modern writers have equated these chakras with specific nerve ganglia in the body, however, the Yogis who first became aware of them saw them as psycho-spiritual centres responsible not only for physical activities but also open to higher or Divine levels of Consciousness.

The outward or physical level of their manifestation is responsible for such activities as excretion and elimination, sexual activities, digestive processes, normal heart rhythm, breathing etc., speech and Conscious thought.

The purpose of chakra meditation is to spiritualise and refine the activities of each centre as only this will ensure perfect health at every level. Normal procedure is to start at the base chakra and ascend a step at a time refining and harmonising each centre.

It is not necessary always to start at the bottom and work upwards, as Consciousness brought down from the higher centres is catalytic in its action, bringing beneficial change without itself getting caught or being involved.

We present here a chakra meditation and lean towards modern psychological terms, it is an integral study which can be approached from either direction. The benefits to be gained are better health, understanding, and co-ordination between each level.

Sahasrara:- The Crown chakra includes everything there is. It is illumined by the vibratory power of spiritual light or angelic fire.

Ajna Chakra:- The Command centre of the Yogis. You should be able to make firm commands based on Truth.
You are the Self, the immanent spirit within. Be careful what you identify with, as you will come under its law.

Vishudda:- The throat chakra is the level of articulate expression. Let the feelings of your heart find expression on your tongue. Love is structured with Truth. When your tongue can express the Truth in your heart there will be an increase of creativity from centre.

Anahata:- This is the heart chakra, the natural centre for feelings of Compassion. This centre feels for all the rest. It is the centre for circulation, and from here all the rest can be fed with the light and Love from the topmost chakras.

Manipura:- This is the level of power demonstration, and pure power does not recognise anything outside of itself. Be Conscious of every act. Let your energy be as a refining fire. When sitting down to eat, your prayer should be – "Let the food I'm about to eat be transformed into a refining energy, and feed those levels which it would feed if I was Self Realised."

Swadisthana:- Your level of sexual enjoyment. By refining this level of activity you do not get less happiness but more. With your partner be nothing less than a God or Goddess, which makes possible a marriage of the highest Truth and Love in Absolute Bliss.

Muladhara:- The level of your survival intent and Self justification. To purify this level of activity be as the Lord of the Earth. Let your actions as far as you are able be a means of encapsulating Truth.

Conclusion

*I*n reality there cannot be any conclusion to this treasury of meditations. Its purpose has been to expand Consciousness and lift the practitioner to ever greater levels of Self Awareness.

Traditionalists will advocate that meditation should be more disciplined, with meditators sitting in straight lines, or facing a wall, hour after hour, ultimately face to face with nothing but themselves.

This is fine for the experienced but hardly suitable for the beginner, who is likely to be put off by what appears to be boring and painful procedures as legs try to cope with unfamiliar seated postures. For the beginner meditation needs to be interesting and stimulating, its many benefits self-evident, so that the aspirant is encouraged to continue and eventually accept more disciplined procedures.

Very few at the outset can sustain progress without guidance from someone with more experience. This may mean joining one of the meditation centres which exists in the U.K. and abroad. Some of these are Christian, some Yogic and others Buddhist. These are usually well organised, the latter run and maintained by Buddhist Monks. The atmosphere in such centres is spiritual and well disciplined and provides the ideal situation for sorting out and re-evaluating one's life, as well as for re-charging the batteries.

Not all of these centres spend hours in meditation, as most maintain a healthy balance between work, study and reflection. Unfortunately these centres are like rare jewels on the landscape and few and far between.

There is nothing however to prevent anyone with the right aptitude and with the help of the meditations in this book to start meditating on a regular basis in their own home.

If forming a group for the first time it is best to combine both relaxation and meditation and encourage each member to make a contribution by briefly describing their experience to the rest of the group. If the motive and direction is right the harmony and rapport between those present will eventually speak for itself.

The measure of such groups and meditation centres is their ability to contribute to the health of society, refresh hearts and minds and help each individual to face up to life with a spirit of optimism.

Faith House Yoga and Natural Health Centre,
155, Victoria Road, New Brighton, Merseyside.

The British Wheel of Yoga,
1, Hamilton Place, Boston Road, Sleaford, Lincs.

Yoga for Health Foundation,
Ickwell Bury, Biggleswade, Bedfordshire.

The Yoga Society International,
Marvin, 4, Norwich Avenue, Banford, Rochdale.

The Northern School of Yoga,
Royde House, 41, Northenden Road, Sale, Cheshire.

Manjushri Institute,
Conishead Priory, Ulverston, Cumbria.

Lam Rim Bristol Trust,
12, Victoria Place, Bedminster, Bristol.

Rigpa,
44, St. Paul's Crescent, London NW1 9TN.

Sakya Thinley Rinchen Ling,
27, Lilymead Avenue, Knowle, Bristol.

Samye-Ling Tibetan Centre,
Eskdalemuir, Near Langholm, Dumfriesshire.

Lam Rim Buddhist Centre,
Pentwyn Manor, Penrhos, Raglan, Gwent,
South Wales.

Manjushri London Centre,
10, Finsbury Park Road, London N4.

International Hermeneutic Society,
Tan-y-Garth Hall, Pontfadog, Llangollen,
Clwyd LL20 7AS.

For Christian Meditation and Weekend Retreats,
both Catholic and Protestant newspapers
contain lists of weekend meditation retreats
usually open to all denominations.

Bibliography of Principal Works Consulted

Foundations of Tibetan Mysticism.
   Lama Anagarika Govinda.
   Rider & Co.

The Secret of the Golden Flower.
   C.G. Jung and R. Wilhelm.
   Kegan Paul, Trench and Trubner, 1942.

Letters on Yoga.
   Sri Aurobindo. Sri Aurobindo Ashram.
   Pondicherry. India.

Concentration and Meditation.
   The Buddhist Lodge. London, 1935.

The Spiritual Teachings of Ramana Maharshi.
   Shambhala Publications.

The Upanishads.
   Juan Mascaro.
   Penguin Classics.

The Bhagavad Gita.
   Juan Mascaro.
   Penguin Classics.

YOGA.
   Ernest Wood.
   Penguin Books.

Hatha Yoga Pradipika.
   Kevin and Venika Kingsland.
   Grael Communications.

Aphorisms of Yoga by Bhagwan Shree Patanjali.
   Translated by Shree Purohit Swami.
   Reprinted by permission of Faber & Faber Ltd.